More READY TO SING

14 Thematic Medleys

ONE Easy Rehearsal...Then Ready To Sing

Arranged by Russell Mauldin

Compiled by Dale Mathews

TABLE OF CONTENTS

Companion Products:

Stereo Listening Cassette:	C-5279N
Stereo Accompaniment Track:	TR-3157C
Split-Track Accompaniment:	TRS-3157C
Soprano Rehearsal Cassette:	C-5279S
Alto Rehearsal Cassette:	C-5279A
Tenor Rehearsal Cassette:	C-5279T
Bass Rehearsal Cassette:	C-5279B

Praise Medley

arranged by Russell Mauldin

9
left His home in glo - ry For the cross of Cal - va -
lov - ing arms a - round me, Drew me back in - to the
G/D
D
A7
12
ry. Yes, I'll sing the won-drous sto - ry Of the
way.
Yes, I'll sing the won-drous sto - ry
D
13
15
Christ who died for me, Sing it with the saints in
Of the Christ who died for me, Sing it with
A7
D

18
1.
glo - ry, Gath ered by the crys- tal sea.
the saints in glo - ry, Gath-ered by the crys- tal sea, the crys - tal sea.
3
A7
1. D G/D D
21
2.
sea.
sea, the crys - tal sea.
2. D G/D D D/A C/D D
"Cut-time" feel
accel.
24
"He Keeps Me Singing" Bridgers
Have fun!
There's with - in my heart a mel - o - dy Je - sus whis-pers sweet and
Feast - ing on the rich - es of His grace, Rest-ing 'neath His shelt - 'ring
Oo
(sing words)
G Eaug E7 A9 D D7

27
Oo
low,
Fear not, I am with thee, peace, be still,
wing,
Al - ways look - ing on His smil - ing face,
G
C/D
G
Eaug
E7
A9
30
(sing words)
32
In all of life's ebb and flow.
That is why I shout and sing.
Je - sus, Je - sus,
D7
G
32
33
Je - sus, Sweet - est name I know,
Am7
D7
D
D+7
G
C/D

36
Fills my ev - 'ry long - ing, Keeps me sing - ing as I
G Bm7 G/B C6 Am7 D7
"Since Jesus Came Into My Heart"
McDaniel, Gabriel
39
1. 2.
41
go. go. Since Je - sus came in - to my
G C/D G D♭/E♭ A♭
42
heart, Since Je - sus came in - to my heart. Floods of
A♭7/C D♭ A♭ B♭m/D♭

45
ff
joy o'er my soul like the sea bil - lows roll, Since
ff
Ab Db/Ab Eb/Ab Ab Eb/Ab Ab Db
ff
48
Je - sus came in - to my
Je - sus, Je - sus, Je - sus,
Ab/Eb Eb7sus Eb
50
heart.
Je - sus came in - to my heart.
Ab

Salvation Medley

8
new work be - gun, Sing praise to the Fa - ther and
G/D D G
10
praise to the Son; Saved by the blood of the
D G/D D Bm7 A7 D
12
13
Saved!
Cru - ci - fied One! Glo - ry, I'm saved!
A7 D
13

14
Saved!
Glo - ry, I'm saved! My sins are all par - doned, my
G
A7
16
Saved!
guilt is all gone! Glo - ry, I'm saved!
D G/D D
18
Saved!
Glo - ry, I'm saved! I'm saved by the blood of the
G
A7
D

1.
2.
Cru - ci - fied One!
Cru - ci - fied One!
1. A7
D
2. A7
D
C/D
D7
rit.
(♪ = 184)
G
mf
26
"Saved, Saved!" Scholfield
I've found a

27
Friend who is all to me, His
Bm7 B♭°7 D7/A D7 G Bm7
30
love is ev - er true;
C Am7 G/D Em/C♯
33
34
I love to tell how He
D
34
G Bm7 B♭°7

36
lift - ed me And what His
D7/A D7 G Bm7 C Am7
39
grace can do for you.
G/D A9 D7sus
42
43
Saved by His pow'r di - vine,
Saved, I'm saved!
D7
43
G Bm7 B♭°7 D7/A A7 D7

45
Saved to new life sub - lime! Life now is sweet, and my
Saved, I'm saved
D/F♯ G D7 G
48
joy is com - plete for I'm saved, saved, saved!
C Am G/B C6 G/D D G C/D
ff
51
ff I'm saved, I'm saved! I'm
ff Life now is sweet, and my joy is com - plete.
G C

54
saved, I'm saved!
for I'm
saved,
saved,
Am7
G/B
C6
G/D
D7
57
Cut-time feel
(♪ stays same)
saved!
mf
59
"Such Love" Bishop, Harkness
That God should love a
(melody)
f
G(♪ stays same)
B♭m7
E♭
A♭
A♭/C
60
sin - ner such as I, Should yearn to change my
D♭
A♭
D♭
E♭/D♭
A♭/C
Fm7

62
sor - row in - to bliss, Nor rest till He had
Bb9 Eb7 Ab Ab/C
64
planned to bring me nigh, How won - der - ful is love like
Db Ab Db/F Ab/Eb Eb7
66
f Such
67
love,
this!
f
Such love, such
f
Ab
67

68
Such
love,
won - drous love,
Such love, such
E♭7
D♭/E♭
E♭7
70
won - drous love.
That
God should love a
A♭
E♭/B♭
A♭/C
A♭7
D♭
72
sin - ner such as I;
How
won - der - ful is love like
A♭
E♭7

74
ff Such
75
love!
Such
this!
ff I'm
saved!
ff
A♭
75
ff
76
love!
I'm
saved!
How
won - der - ful
to
know
I'm
B♭/A♭
B♭m7
E♭7sus
E♭7
78
saved!
A♭

Call to Worship Medley

arranged by Russell Mauldin

12
parts
13
eyes. Most bless - ed, most glo - rious the An - cient of
sight; All laud we would ren - der: O help us to
F
13
Dm C/E F Dm Am F
16
1.
Days, Al - might - y, vic - to - rious, Thy great Name we
see 'Tis on - ly the splen - dor of
C F B♭ Gm C Dm
1. F/C C7
20
2.
Rall.
praise. Thou light hid - eth Thee.
F
2. F/C C7
Rall.
F (♩ = 88) N.C.

24
27
O for a thou - sand
Dsus
D
G/B G D
28
tongues to sing My great Re - deem - er's praise, The
G D Em D G D7/F♯ G D
31
glo - ries of my God and King, The triumphs of His
G G/B C G/D D7

34
35
grace. My gracious Master and my God, As-
G G/F E♭7 A♭/C A♭ E♭ A♭ E♭ Fm E♭
37
sist me to pro - claim, To spread thro' all the
A♭ E♭7/G A♭ E♭ E♭/G E♭ A♭ A♭/C
40
rit.
ff Broadly
earth a - broad, The hon - ors of Thy name. O
D♭ A♭/E♭ E♭7 A♭ E♭ /D♭
rit.

43 [43] *a tempo*

wor - ship the King, all glo - rious a - bove, And

[43] Ab/C Eb Ab Db/F Eb7/G Ab Eb Eb7

a tempo

47

grate - ful - ly sing His pow'r and His

Ab Ab/C Eb Ab Db/F Ab/C Ab/Eb Eb7

50 *mp* [51] *cresc. poco a poco*

love; Our shield and De - fen - der, the

mp

Ab [51] Eb Bb7/Eb Eb7 Ab/Eb

mp

cresc. poco a poco

53
ff
An - cient of Days, Pa - vil - ioned in splen - dor and
ff
E♭ A♭/E♭ E♭7 A♭ A♭/C E♭ A♭ D♭/F
ff
57
gird - ed with praise, with
A♭/E♭ E♭ E♭7 A♭ D♭/A♭ E♭7
61
praise!
A♭

Christian Life Medley

arranged by Russell Mauldin

9
in a song with sweet ac - cord,
Join in a song with
G C/G G Am7/C Am7 D G/D D
12
And thus sur - round the throne, And
sweet ac - cord.
A7 D G D G7 Am/C
15
f
17
thus sur - round the throne. We're march - ing to
G/D Em/D D7 G G

18
Zi - on, Beau - ti - ful, beau - ti - ful Zi - on; We're
D7
21
march - ing up - ward to Zi - on, the beau - ti - ful ci - ty of
G C Am7 G/B Am/C G/D D7
24
1.
God. We're
2.
God. The beau - ti - ful ci - ty of
1. G
2. G C Am7 G/D D7

"I Feel Like Traveling On"
Hunter
27
Brightly mf
29
God.
My heav - 'n'ly home is
(The) Lord has been so
Brightly (♩ = 92)
G
C/D
29
G
30
bright and fair, I feel like trav - el - ing on. Nor
good to me, Un -
D7
C6/D
33
pain nor death can en - ter there, I feel like trav - el - ing
til that bless - ed home I see,
G
G/D
D7

36
37
on. Yes, I feel like trav - el - ing on, I
trav - el - ling on,
G
D G
39
feel like trav - el - ing on. My heav - 'n'ly home is
A9
D
C/D
G
42
1.
bright and fair, I feel like trav - el - ing on. The
G/D
D7
1. G
C/D

"Higher Ground"
Oatman, Gabriel
45
2.
47
on.
Lord, lift me up and let me
Lord, lift me up
2. G G/F C/E D♭/E♭
A♭ (♩ = 96)
poco accel.
mp
f
48
stand, By faith, on heav - en's ta-ble-land, A high-er
By faith on heav-en's
E♭7
A♭
51
plane than I have found; Lord, plant my feet on high-er
1.
E♭/B♭ A♭/C D♭ B♭m7
1. A♭/E♭ E♭7

54
2.
ground. Lord, lift me feet on high - er
A♭
2. A♭/E♭
E♭7
57
ff
ground, On high - er
A♭
D♭/A♭
A♭7
D♭
59
ground!
ground, On high - er ground!
A♭

Consecration Medley

arranged by Russell Mauldin

10
love and trust Him, In His pres - ence dai - ly live.
love and pow - er, Let Thy bless - ing fall on me.
G/B E7/G♯ Am F/A Am7 G7sus G13 C F/G
13
13
mf
I sur - ren - der all, I sur - ren - der
mf
C Am/C G/C Dm Dm/C G/B F/A G F/G Em/G G9
mf
16
all, All to Thee my bless - ed Sav - ior,
C F/G G13 C F/C C C/E G/F F

19
1.
I sur - ren - der all.
C/G F/G C/G G7
1. C F/C C G/B F6/A Gsus G
22
2.
all.
mf
I am
(mel.)
mf
Slight accel.
2.C F/A Am7 D7sus D7 G
25
"I Am Thine, O Lord"
Crosby, Doane
Thine O Lord, I have heard Thy voice, And it told Thy love to
N.C. G C

28
me; But I long to rise in the arms of faith, And be
G G/D D D♯o7 Em Dm11 G7
31
(S.A.)
33
clos - er drawn to Thee. Draw me near - er,
Draw me near - er,
Am7 D7 G C/D
33
G G/B
34
near-er bless-ed Lord, To the cross where Thou hast died; Draw me
C G G/B Bm7 C Am7 G/A D C/D

37
mp
near - er, near - er, near - er bless - ed Lord, To Thy
mp
G
G/B
C
Cm6
40
1.
f
2.
pre - cious bleed - ing side. Draw me pre - cious
f
1.G/D
D13
G
C/D
2.G/D
Em7
43
accel.
bleed - ing side.
Am9
D13
A♭Maj7/B♭
B♭9
A♭Maj7/B♭
B♭9
accel.

46
48
mp
Have Thine own
mp
(♩ = 84)
E♭2
48
mp
49
way, Lord! Have Thine own
A♭/E♭
E♭
52
way.
Search me and
Fm/E♭
B♭9/D
B♭7
B♭°7
B♭7

55
try me, Mas - ter to -
Gm/B♭
B♭7
B♭7
A♭/B♭
B♭7
58
60
mf
day!
Whit - er than
E♭
A♭Maj7/B♭
B♭9
61
snow, Lord, Wash me just
A♭/E♭
E♭
E♭7
E♭°7
E♭7

64
f
now,
As in Thy
f
A♭
B♭/A♭
A♭
f
67
mf
pres - ence
Hum - bly I
mf
Gm7
Cm
B♭7
A♭/B♭
B♭7
70
71
f
bow.
As in Thy pres -
f
E♭
71
A♭
B♭/A♭
A♭
Gm7
f

73
mf
Slight rall.
ence
Hum - bly I
mf
Cm
Bb7
Ab/Bb
Bb7
mf
Slight rall.
76
76
bow.
Hum - bly at His
All to Je - sus I sur - ren - der,
76
Eb
Ab/C Cm7
Bb/D
G/B
Cm
Ab/C Cm7
79
mp
rit.
feet I bow.
mp
Ab6/Bb Bb13
Eb
Ab/C Cm7
Bb7sus
Bb7
Eb2
rit.

Blood of Jesus Medley

arranged by Russell Mauldin

9
saved the worst a - mong you, When He
For He saved the worst a - mong you, worst a - mong you,
C/G G
11
saved a wretch like me.
f
And I
When He saved a wretch like me, a wretch like me.
D G C/G G G/B
13
13
know, yes, I know, Jesus'
Je - sus'
f I sure - ly know, I sure - ly know,
13
Am7 D9 G

15
blood can make the vil - est sin - ner clean. And I
D7
G
17
know, yes, I know, Jesus'
I sure - ly know, I sure - ly know,
Am7
D9
G
19
mf
blood can make the vil - est sin - ner clean. Have you
(Are you)
mf
D7
G
E♭7
f

"Are You Washed In the Blood?" Hoffman
21
21
been to Je - sus for the cleans - ing pow'r? Are you
walk - ing dai - ly by the Sav - ior's side?
A♭ D♭/A♭ A♭ D♭/A♭ A♭
21
mf
23
washed in the blood of the Lamb? Are you
Do you
Fm7 E♭ D♭/E♭
25
ful - ly trust - ing in His grace this hour? Are you
rest each mo - ment in the Cru - ci - fied?
A♭ A♭7/C D♭ Fm7/C B♭m7 E♭7

27
f
washed in the blood of the Lamb? Are you
Ab Ab/Eb Eb7 Ab
f
29
29
washed in the blood, In the
f Are you washed in the blood,
29
Db
31
soul - cleans - ing blood of the Lamb? Are your
Ab Ab/C Eb Ab Eb Db/Eb

33
garments spotless? Are they white as snow? Are you
A♭ A♭7/C D♭ Fm7/C B♭m7 E♭
35
1. 2.
washed in the blood of the Lamb? Are you Lamb?
A♭ A♭/E♭ E♭7 1. A♭ 2. A♭
ff
38
A♭/E♭ B♭/F Fsus F

41
"There Is Power In the Blood" Jones
mf Would you be free from the burden of sin?
f There's
Bb Bb7 Eb Bb
mf
43
pow'r in the blood,
f Won - der - work - ing pow'r in the blood.
pow'r in the blood.
F7 Bb
45
mf Would you o'er e - vil a vic - to - ry win?
f There's
Bb7 Eb Bb

47
49
won - der- ful pow'r in the blood. There is pow'r, pow'r,
Pow'r, pow'r,
F7
B♭
49
B♭
B♭7
f
50
won - der - work - ing pow'r in the blood of the
won - der - work - ing pow'r in the blood of the
E♭
B♭
F
52
Lamb. There is pow'r, pow'r,
Lamb. Pow'r, pow'r,
B♭
B♭7

54
won - der - work - ing pow'r in the pre - cious
won - der - work - ing pow'r
E♭
B♭
Cm7
56
1.
ff
blood of the Lamb. And there's still
1. F6
F7
B♭
Fsus
F
ff
59
2.
ff
blood of the Lamb. Won - der - work - ing pow'r!
There is pow'r, pow'r,
2. F6
E♭/F
B♭
N.C.
B♭

Guidance Medley

arranged by Russell Mauldin

10
11
home? mf When Je - sus is my por-tion? My
C FMaj7/G G7 C G7/D C/E Dm11 Dm11/C G/B
mf
13
con - stant Friend is He; His eye is on the
C G7/D C/E F(2-1) A7/E Dm Dm/C G/B G/F
16
f
spar - row, And I know He watch - es me; His
C/E G/A Am Dm11 G/B C F/G G
f
19
mp
eye is on the spar - row, And I know He watch - es
B♭9/C C/B♭ F(2-1)/A Am7 A♭Maj7 Fm6/A♭ C/G G6 G7
mp

22
23
f
me. I sing be - cause I'm hap - py, I
C
G7
C
25
sing be - cause I'm free, For His eye is on the
G7
C
B♭9/C
C/B♭
28
mf
1.
spar-row And I know He watch - es me. I
F(2-1)/A
Am7
A♭Maj7
Fm6/A♭
C/G
G6
G7
C(2-1)
C(2-1)

2.
know He watch - es me.
know, yes, I know
2. C/G
FMaj7/G
G
C(2-1)
C/B
35
"God Leads Us Along" Young
In shad - y green pas - tures so
C/B♭
A7sus A7 G/A
D
D°
D
rich and so sweet, God leads His dear chil - dren a -
Bm7 A7
Bm/A A7

38
long; Where the wa - ter's cool flow bathes the
D GMaj7/A A7 G/A D D° D
40
God leads His dear chil-dren a - long.
wea - ry one's feet.
Bm7 A7 D G/A A/G
f
43
43
f
Some thro' the wa-ters, some thro' the flood, Some thro' the fire, but
f
43
D/F♯ D7 G D F♯m7 Bm7

46
all thro' the Blood; Some thro' great sor-row, but God gives a song,
E9 A A/G D/F♯ D7 G D
49
mf
In the night sea - son and all the day long.
mf
D/A Bm B♭7(♭5) A7 G/A A7 D G/A
51
51
In the night sea-son and all the day long.
Molto Rit. ff
He
ff
51
D/A Bm B♭7(♭5) A7 G/A A7 D G/A A/G
ff
Molto Rit.

54
54 (♩ = 84) Broadly
lead - eth me, He lead - eth
(♩ = 84) Broadly
54 D/F♯ D A/C♯ A/G D/F♯ A9/G
57
me, By His own hand He
D G D(2-1-Maj7)/A Bm9 B♭7(♭5)
60
lead - eth me: His
D/A Asus A/G

63
63
faith - ful fol - l'wer I would
63
D/F♯ D A/C♯ A/G D/F♯ A9/G
66
mf
be, For by His hand He
mf
D G D(2-1-Maj7)/A Bm9 B♭7(♭5)
69
mp
lead - eth Some thro' great sor - row, but
mp
me.
D/A Asus A D D/C
mp

73
75
Stagger breathing
God gives a song, And by His
G/B
D/A
G
75
D(2-1-Maj7)
76
hand He lead - eth
Bm9
B♭7(♭5)
D/A
Asus
A
79
Rit.
me.
Dsus
D
Rit.

Stand Medley

9
high His roy - al ban - ner, It must not suf - fer
arm of flesh will fail you Ye dare not trust your
B♭ B♭7/D E♭ B♭ B♭/D B♭/F F7
12
(Parts both times)
13
loss; From vic - t'ry un - to vic - t'ry His
own; Put on the gos - pel ar - mor, Each
B♭
13
F B♭ B♭/A♭
15
ar - my shall He lead, Till ev - 'ry foe is
piece put on with pray'r Where du - ty calls or
E♭/G B♭/F E♭ Cm7 B♭/F F7 B♭ B♭7/D

18
van - quished And Christ is Lord in - deed.
dan - ger, Be nev - er want - ing there.
E♭ B♭ B♭/D B♭/F F7 B♭
21
1.
(Parts)
Stand
2.
1B♭/D E♭2 B♭/D Fsus F
2B♭/F B♭/A♭
24
Unison choir 26
"Lead On, O King Eternal"
Shurtleff, Smart
Lead on, O King E -
C/G Gsus G F/G G
26
C F/C

27
ter - nal, We fol - low not with fears; For
C C/B♭ F/A C/G F G7sus G
30
glad - ness breaks like morn - ing Wher - e'er Thy face ap -
C F/C C G/D D7
33
Slight accel.
34
pears; Thy cross is lift - ed o'er us; We
G G/F C/E G7/D C C/E F F/E♭
Slight accel.

36
journey - ney in its light; The crown a - waits the
D
D/F♯
G
G/F
C/E
Dm7/F
C7/G
39
con - quest; Lead on, O God of might.
F
G/F
F
C/G
G7
C
42
43
"Sound the Battle Cry!" Sherwin
Rall.
a tempo
mf
Sound the bat - tle cry! See, the foe is nigh;
B♭m9
E♭7
A♭
D♭
A♭
Rall.
mf a tempo

45
mf
Gird your ar - mor on;
Raise the stan-dard high For the Lord;
E♭ A♭/E♭ E♭
B♭7
E♭7
A♭
48
Stand firm, ev-'ry one; Rest your cause up-on His ho - ly Word.
D♭ A♭
Cm7 Fm7
D♭m6/E
A♭/E♭ E♭7 A♭
f
51
51
f
Rouse, then, sol-diers, ral - ly 'round the ban - ner; Ready-y, stead-y,
f
51
A♭
A♭/C
E♭7
E♭°7
E♭9
A♭
C7
Fm

54
pass the word a - long;
On - ward, for - ward
B♭7
E♭7
A♭
A♭/C
56
shout a - loud Ho - san - na!
Christ is Cap - tain of the
E♭7
E○7
E♭9
A♭
A♭
Cm7
Fm
D♭m6/F♭
58
might - y throng.
59
ff
Christ is
ff
A♭/E♭
E♭7
A♭
59
A♭
Cm7
ff

60
Cap - tain of the might - y
Fm
D♭m6/F♭
A♭/E♭
E♭/G
E♭
62
throng. Stand up! Stand
A♭
A♭7
D♭
64
up for Je - sus!
E♭/A♭
A♭

Testimony Medley

arranged by Russell Mauldin

5

Ab Eb/G Bb/D Fm/Eb Eb Bb Ab/Bb

low in the pit where my sins dragged me down; I
day and by night its sweet notes I will raise; My

7

Eb Eb/Db Ab/C Ab

cried to the Lord from the deep mir - y
heart's o - ver - flow - ing, I'm hap - py and

9

Cm/A Eb/Bb Cm7

clay, Who ten - der - ly bro't me out to
free, I'll praise my Re - deem - er, who has

mp *ff* *f*

11 **12** *f*

golden day. He bro't me out of the mir-y clay,
res-cued me.

Fm9 Bb7 Eb **12** Ab Eb Bb/D

14

He set my feet on the Rock to stay;

Cm F7 Bb Ab/Bb Bb Ab/Bb

16

He puts a song in my soul to-day, A

Eb Eb/Db Ab/C Ab Cm/A

mf *ff*

19
1.
2.
song of praise, hal-le - lu - jah. lu - jah.
Eb/Bb Cm7
1. Fm7 Bb7 Eb
2. Fm7 Bb7 Eb
22
24
"Joy Unspeakable" Warren
I have found His grace is
mf
Eb6/F F7
(♩ = 100)
Bb Bb/D
accel.
mf
25
mf
all com - plete. He sup - pli - eth ev' - ry need; While I
Eb Bb F F7

28
sit and learn at Je - sus' feet, I am free, yes, free in -
B♭ B♭/D E♭ B♭ F/C Gm/C F/C C7
31
f
32
deed. It is joy un - speak - a - ble and full of glo - ry,
F7
B♭ E♭/B♭ B♭
34
Full of glo - ry, full of glo - ry; It is joy un - speak - a - ble and
F B♭ F6 B♭ E♭/B♭

37
1.
full of glo-ry, Oh the half has nev - er yet been told. Oh yes it's
B♭ B♭/D E♭ Cm7F7sus F7 E♭/FF7
1. B♭ F7
ff
40
2.
told.
2. B♭
B♭6/C
C7
accel.
"How Can I Forget?" (Author unknown)
1st time: Unison
2nd time: Parts
43
f
How can I for - get what He's done for me? How can I for - get how He
(♩ = 106)
F F7 B♭ F B♭/C F Dm7

Parts both times
46
set me free? How can I— for - get what He's
G7 C7 F F7
48
done for me? How can I— for - get? No
B♭ F F/A B♭ F/C
50
1. 2.
nev - er! nev - er!
1. C7 F 2. C7 F

52
How can I for - get? No
F/C
B♭
F/A
Dm7
54
nev - er!
Gm7
C7
56
ff
How can I for - get what He's done for me?
F
gliss

Worship Medley

Flowing (♩=90)

arranged by Russell Mauldin

10
free that I might praise Thy name.
E♭7
B♭m7
E♭7
A♭(2-1)
D♭/E♭
13
13
Let all bond - age go, and let de - liv - 'rance
13
A♭
E♭/D♭
D♭
16
flow. Set my spir - it free to wor - ship
B♭m7
F7/A
B♭m
E♭7

19
1.
(to parts)
2.
Thee.
Thee.
1. A♭
E♭7/G E♭7
2. A♭
E♭/A♭
"My Soul Doth Magnify the Lord" Clark*
23
Warmly
mf
25
Rall.
My soul doth mag - ni - fy the
mf
(♩ =69)
Gm11
C7sus C7
25
F2
F
Rall.
26
Lord. My soul doth mag - ni - fy the
Gm/F
F2
F

28
Lord. My spir - it re - joic - es in
A♭(2-1-Maj7) Csus C F/A
B♭Maj9 B♭6 B♭m/G
30
God my Sav - ior, for my soul doth mag - ni - fy the
F/C Dm7
Gm7 B♭Maj7/C C7
32
1. Lord. My 2. Lord. For my soul doth mag - ni - fy the
1. F B♭/C C
2. F Dm7
Gm7 B♭Maj7/C C7sus C7

"In Your Presence"
Gordon*
37
35
Lord.
In Your
pres - ence, Lord,
F2
F
G/A
A
G/A
(♩=80)
D2
D
f
38
there is
splen - dor.
In Your
D(2-1)
Em11
Em7
A7
B7aug
B7
41
pres - ence, Lord,
we sur - ren - der.
Em
G6/A
A7
Em/D
D

44
45
In Your pres - ence, Lord, we bow be -
Em/D
Am7
D7
Bm/D
D9
47
fore You to a - dore You,
C/G
G
Em7
F♯m/A
Em/A
D/A
50
to be - hold You as Lord and
Bm7
Em/B
Bm7
Em7
G/A
A7

53
1.
King.
In Your
1. D
Em/D
55
2.
King.
Lord and
2. D
Em/D
57
rit.
King.
D2
D
rit.

Resurrection Medley

arranged by Russell Mauldin

8
thrilled me day by day. They told me how He suf - fered and
D A7 D7 G
10
died on Cal - va - ry; And though I knew that it was true, I
Em7 D/F♯ G C D♭°7 G/D Em
12
Choir f
13
That He's a - live and the
want - ed now to see. He's a - live
G/D D7 G G C/G G
f

14
tomb is emp - ty now! He rose a - gain by His
rose a - gain
Em D/F♯ G C/G G
16
grand tri - um - phant pow'r, He's seat - ed now at the
seat - ed now
A13 D7 G C/G G
18
Fa - ther's own right hand; The war is won and He's a -
the work is done,
B7 B7/D♯ Em C G/B C C/D

1st time: Unison Choir
2nd time: Parts
20
live!
Don't look for
G C/G G
A♭Maj7/B♭ B♭13
22 "Don't Look for Him in the Grave" Mathews*
Him in the grave He is gone. Don't look for Him in the grave He is a -
E♭ Fm7 E♭/G A♭Maj7/B♭ B♭13 E♭ Cm7
25
Parts both times
live; death has been de - nied. Don't look for
Tho' He was cru - ci - fied,
Fm11 B♭13 E♭ E♭/G A♭ Fm7 E♭/G A♭

28

1. (Parts)

2. Unison choir

Him in the grave He is gone. Don't look for gone. A -

Eb/Bb Bb13 1. Eb AbMaj7/Bb Bb13 2. Eb Bb/C C

"Alive, Alive" Traditional

31 **31**

live, a - live, a - live for - ev - er - more; My Je - sus is a - live, a -

31 F F/A Bb F C F/G C7

34

live for - ev - er - more. A - live, a - live, a - live for - ev - er - more; My

F BbMaj7/C Bbadd9/C F F/A Bb F

37
Parts
Je - sus is a - live. Sing hal - le -
C7 F/G C7 F Gm7 F7/A
39
39
lu - jah, Sing hal - le - lu - jah, My Je - sus is a -
B♭ F C
42
live for - ev - er - more. Sing hal - le - lu - jah, Sing hal - le - lu - jah, My
F F/A B♭ F

45
1.
ff
2.
Je - sus is a - live. Sing hal-le– live. Sing hal-le-
ff
C
1. F F7/A
2. F F7/A
ff
48
48
lu - jah! He is a -
48
B♭
50
live!
B♭/F F

By and By Medley

arranged by Russell Mauldin

5
ways that God would lead us to that bless-ed Prom-ised Land; But He
Dm7
G7
C
B♭/C
7
(Parts)
mf
guides us with His eye, and we'll fol-low till we die, For we'll
mf
F
F7/A
B♭6
F
9
accel.
"Cut-time" feel
11
mf
un-der-stand it bet-ter by and by. By and by
mf
"Cut-time" feel
(♩ = 100)
Dm7
Gm7
C13
F
B♭/F
F
11
F
B♭/F
F
F7
accel.
f

12
when the morn - ing comes, When the saints of
B♭ F F Dm7
14
God are gath - ered home, We'll tell the sto - ry
G C C13 F F7
16
how we've o - ver - come, For we'll un - der - stand it bet - ter by and
B♭ F Dm7 Gm7 C13

19
"In the Sweet By and By" Bennett, Webster
by. In the sweet by and
In the sweet by and
F Bb/F F
F Dm7
by, We shall meet on that beau - ti - ful
by,
Gm7 C Bb6 F/A
Gm7 C9
shore; In the sweet by and
In the sweet by and
F Bb/C
F F7/A

24
by, We shall meet on that beau - ti - ful shore. In the
by,
B♭ Gm7 C B♭/C F C F D
27
27
sweet by and by, We shall
In the sweet by and by,
G Em7 Am D C6 G/B
29
meet on that beau - ti - ful shore; In the
Am7 D9 G C/D

31
sweet
In the sweet by and by,
by and by, by and by,
G
G9/B
C
Em/C♯
33
We shall meet on that beau - ti - ful shore!
C♯°7
mp
ff
G/D
D7sus
D7
G
36
37
"When the Roll Is Called Up Yonder" Black
(Opt. solo)
mf
When the trum - pet of the Lord shall sound and
37
G
G7
mf

38
time shall be no more, And the morn - ing breaks e - ter - nal, bright and
C G Em A9/C♯
40
fair; When the saved of earth shall gath - er o - ver
Am7 D G G7
42
on the oth - er shore, And the roll is called up yon - der I'll be
C G G/D D7

44
(Choir)
45
When the roll is called up
there. When the roll is called up
G C/G G
45
46
yon - der, When the roll is called up
yon - der I'll be there. When the roll is called up
D7
48
yon - der, When the roll is called up
yon - der I'll be there.
G G7

50
yon - der, When the roll is called up yon - der I'll be
C
Am7
G/D
D7
52
53
there.
When the roll is called up
When the roll is called up
G G/F D♭/E♭
A♭
54
yon-der I'll be there.
yon - der, When the roll is called up
When the roll is called up
E♭7

56
yon - der I'll be there. When the roll is called up
yon - der,
A♭ A♭7
58
yon - der, When the
D♭ D♭m/B♭
60
roll is called up
A♭/E♭ A♭aug/E♭ A♭6/E♭ A♭7/E♭

62
yon - der
I'll be
Bbm7
Db/Eb
64
there!
I'll be
Ab
Gb9
66
there!
Ab
8va

Holy Spirit Medley

arranged by Russell Mauldin

8
day? Claim the prom - ise of your Fa - ther, come ac -
still; And ac - cord - ing to His prom - ise with the
A7
Em7
A7
10
cord - ing to His Word In the bless - ed old - time
Ho - ly Ghost and pow'r, He will ev - 'ry ves - sel
D
D6
A/E
E7
12
f
13
way.
fill. He will fill your heart to - day to o - ver -
A
A/G
D/F♯
A7/E
D
G

14
flow - ing, As the Lord com-mand-eth you,
flow-ing, o-ver-flow-ing, "Bring your
D
A
16
He will fill your heart to-day to o-ver-
ves-sels not a few." fill your
D
D7/F♯
G
18
flow - ing, with the Ho - ly Ghost and
heart to o - ver - flow - ing
D
Bm7
D/A
G
D/A
A7

20

1. pow'r. *mf* Like the 2. pow'r. The

1. D 2. D D/C A♭/B♭ B♭7

22 "Waiting on the Lord" Weigle

pow - er! The pow - er! Gives

22 E♭ (♩ = 98) Gm7 A♭ E♭

24

vic - t'ry o - ver sin and pu - ri - ty with - in; The

E♭/B♭ B♭ B♭9/D A♭/E♭ E♭ A♭/B♭

26
pow - er! The pow - er! The
E♭ Gm7 A♭ E♭
28
pow'r they had at Pen - te - cost.
E♭/B♭ Fm7 B♭7 E♭
30
Unison choir
mf
I'm re -
mf
Cadd9/D D7

32 *"He Abides"* *Buffam, Shanks*

32

joic - ing night and day, As I walk the pil - grim way, For the

32 G (♩ = 100) G7 C6 Am7

mf

34

hand of God in all my life I see, and the

D7 G Am7 D7

36

rea - son of my bliss, Yes, the se - cret all is this: That the

mf

(mel.)

G G7 C6 Am7

38
Com - fort - er a - bides with me. He a -
D7 D6 D7 G Am7 CMaj7/D D9
40
40
bides, He a - bides, Hal - le -
40
G Bm7 Em7 G2/D G2/B
42
lu - jah He a - bides with me. I'm re - joic-ing night and day, As I
Am7 D7 G Am7 D7 G G7

45
For the Com - fort - er a - bides with
walk the nar - row way,
C6
Am7
D7
D6
D7
47
1.
2.
ff
49
me.
He a–
me.
He a - bides,
He a -
1. G
Am7
CMaj7/D
D9
2. G
Am7
CMaj7/D
D9
49
G
50
bides,
He a - bides!
C
Cm6
G

Witness Medley

arranged by Russell Mauldin

10
vol - un - teers to serve Him near and far. Lord,
A♭ A°7 E♭/B♭ B♭13 E♭ A♭/B♭
13
13
lay some soul up - on my heart, And love that soul thro'
13
E♭ B♭13 Fm7/E♭ E♭ B♭ Cm7 B♭7/D
16
f
me; And may I ev - er do my part to
f
E♭ B♭m7 E♭7/G A♭ A°7 E♭/B♭ Cm A♭m6/C♭
f

19
mf
21
win that soul for Thee. To win some soul for
Eb/Bb Ab/Bb Bb13 Eb Ab/Bb Eb Bb6
22
Thee, To win some soul for Thee, And
f
Eb Bb Cm7 Bb7/D Eb Bbm7 Eb7/G
25
may I ev - er do my part to win some
Ab A°7 Eb/Bb Cm Abm6/Cb Eb/Bb Fm/Bb

28
soul for Thee.
Gm/B♭ Fm/B♭ E♭ A♭/E♭
31
"Let the Beauty of Jesus"
Osborn, Jones
33
Let the
Subito faster
(♪ =160)
E♭ E♭ E♭/B♭
34
beau - ty of Je - sus be seen in me,
E♭ E♭/B♭ E♭ B♭7 E♭

37
All His won-der-ful pas-sion and pu - ri -
Fm Caug7 Fm7 A♭/B♭ B♭9
40
41
ty;
Oh, Thou Spir-it di-vine,
E♭
E♭ B♭7sus/F B♭7/F B♭7
43
All my na-ture re-fine Till the
A♭/E♭ E♭ E♭° E♭
B♭7/F

46
beau - ty of Je - sus be seen in me.
1.
Eb/G Ab Eb/Bb Bb13 Bb7
1Eb
49
2.
me.
"Jesus, the Son of God" Traditional
mf
Do
2Eb Eb7
(♩ =112) Ab
"Swing feel"
mf
52
52
you know Je - sus, Our Lord, our
52
Ab/C Db

55
Sav - ior, Je - sus, the Son of
D♭/A♭ A♭
Fm7
58
60
God?
Have you ev - er
E♭ B♭7/F E♭ E♭/D♭
60
C7
61
seen Him, or shared of His fa - vor?
Fm A♭7/E♭ D♭ D♭/A♭ A♭

64
Je - sus, the Son of God?
Fm
E♭13
E♭7
A♭
D♭/A♭
A♭
68
68
O sweet Won - der! O sweet
68
A♭/C
D♭
71
Won - der! Je - sus, the Son of
D♭/A♭ A♭
Fm7

74
God;
76
How I a -
Eb Bb7/F Eb Eb/Db
76
C7
77
dore Thee!
O how I love Thee!
Fm Ab7/Eb Db Db/Ab Ab
80
Je - sus, the Son of
Fm Eb13 Eb7

82
God.
A♭
D♭/A♭
A♭
84
84
O
sweet
Won
-
der!
84
mp
86
molto rit.
mp
O
sweet
Won
-
der!
mp
D♭
B♭m7
D♭/A♭
A♭
molto rit.